Champagne & Sparkling Wine

Champagne & Sparkling Wine

◆

grape goddess® guides to good living

Advice decadently laced with juicy insider tips, anecdotes, and real-life experience from a world-renowned Master Sommelier, bon vivant, and lover of luxury in all its forms.

by Catherine Fallis, Master Sommelier

Annie,
May the sensual pleasures of wine enrich your daily life.
Catherine Fallis MS
aka
grape goddess

iUniverse, Inc.
New York Lincoln Shanghai

Champagne & Sparkling Wine
grape goddess® guides to good living

iUniverse, Inc.

For information address:
iUniverse, Inc.
2021 Pine Lake Road, Suite 100
Lincoln, NE 68512
www.iuniverse.com

ISBN: 0-595-32702-8

Printed in the United States of America

Thank you to my Nana, the late Lucille Leone Kendall, who provided unending love and nourishment for my body and soul when no one else would. She was my rock.

Thank you to my Nana, too, for teaching me to chew with my mouth shut, thus making me aware of manners and etiquette for the first time. Her spirit lives on in me.

Thank you to my soul mate and baby brother, the late Sidney Fallis, a constant source of inspiration to me. He was an artist in so many senses of the word, an entrepreneur, and an amazing Dad. His spirit lives on in his sons, my nephews, who constantly amaze me with the same joyful song, dance, and clowning around that filled the house when he was alive.

Thank you to my sister-in-law and her husband for providing such a loving home to the boys.

Thank you to my brother Christopher Kendall Fallis and his wife for providing love, support, general advice, and life lessons on being a foster parent. Thank you to their children, my niece and nephew, for giving me renewed appreciation for the single life.

Thank you to my brother Alex for cheering me on and providing unending witty commentary.

Thank you to my brother James for showing such strength of character. Thank you to my sister, Christina, for having the courage to take the plunge into the culinary world.

To Kevin Zraly, I thank you from the bottom of my heart for believing in me.

Writing is a solitary activity requiring great concentration. To my neglected friends and family members, I thank you for your understanding and patience.

Contents

Preface

A magical elixir, Champagne teases then pleases the senses. Hands caress the shapely bottle then, with a twist and a pop, masterfully unleash the bubbling potion within. Glasses filled with shimmering gold are clinked together, adding to the soft, fizzing sound of the bubbles. Noses crinkle as bubbles jump up to greet and tickle them. The seduction is complete as tickling, teasing bubbles merge with pleasing flavors on the palate. A feeling of lightheadedness sets in, giving rise, with refortification, to silly, wanton behavior. Is there any other beverage in the solar system that gives as much brio to the spirit, body, heart, and soul as Champagne?

La Dolce Vita

Burgundy makes you think of silly things, Bordeaux makes you talk of them, and Champagne makes you do them.

—Jean Anthelme Brillat-Savarin

The salient points of my adult life are easily chronicled with Champagne.

I am visiting the Champagne region for the first time on a weekend jaunt from the American College in Paris, where I am in my junior year learning about European culture, with a major in food and men. I find myself hugging a huge display bottle outside of a shop in Reims, holding on for dear life, not wanting to part with the magic it promises.

I am visiting Taittinger, and I am charged for the tasting at the very end, without warning. I try to explain that I am a hospitality student on a budget and I am served up a huge dish of attitude. I vow never to drink Taittinger again.

I am back in the states trying to bond with my biological mother, sitting in her kitchen with a bottle of Mumm Extra Dry, naively thinking we could become closer.

I am hanging out with other sommeliers behind the scenes at a wine event at the Hilton Hawaiian Village, in Waikiki. My hunky blue-eyed boyfriend is drinking Krug Grand Cuvée from my red leather stiletto pump, his eyes shining and full of mischief. My mind keeps drifting back to the vision of him, muscles rippling, in a Speedo.

I am tasting the rare, exquisite Philopponnat Clos de Goisses 1983 with the tall drink of water who is the sommelier at the Halekulani Hotel, knowing immediately that this would be the benchmark by which I judged all other Champagnes.

A decade later, we are at a sommelier gathering at a somewhat less balmy California beach. We stumble into the hospitality suite after dinner and order double magnums of Bollinger RD and charge them someone else's room. By this time, I am a Master Sommelier.

The Master Sommelier Diploma, granted by the UK-based Court of Master Sommeliers, is the ultimate professional credential that anyone can attain worldwide. The MS syllabus includes production methods of wines and spirits, international wine laws, harmony of food and wine, wine-tasting skills, and practical service and salesmanship, including service of liqueurs, brandies, ports, and cigars. In a blind tasting of six wines in twenty-five minutes, candidates must correctly identify grape varieties, country and region of origin, age, and quality. Hundreds begin but very few candidates successfully complete the programs. 110 have earned the title, of which only 11 are women. Visit www.courtofmastersommeliers.org for more information.

I am working in Los Angeles, selling Mumm Champagne, working the market with Mumm Ambassador Paul Bocuse. We are at the Four Seasons Beverly Hills sipping Mumm Grand Cordon with famous chef and genuinely nice guy Wolfgang Puck. I deliver cases of Mumm to the studio lots. I attend movie premiere parties and rub shoulders with the handsome hunk and complete sweetheart Brad Pitt, the standoffish Kevin Costner, the engaging Arnold Schwarzenegger, and the sweet-as-pie, larger-than-life Dolly Parton.

I am living in Malibu, toasting to my ripped hard-bodied kiwi lover as the sun sets over the Pacific. Earlier we'd jogged barefoot in the sand alongside Olivia Newton-John. I am on holiday in Monaco with a handsome young French sommelier. We are tearing up the winding roads in his little red convertible, Barry White blasting. Everywhere we go, we are offered Champagne. His friends bring him the sword. After a while, I want to try. Finally I do it, and I am hooked. Thrill junkie finds a new drug! I research, practice, and become a professional *sabreur*. I stand in the gardens of the French Laundry, my ivory silk heels sinking into mud. The sun is directly in my eyes. I can barely see through my Chanel shades. Sweat is running down my back. I am petrified of screwing up in front of Chef Thomas Keller. The entire kitchen crew is on the balcony looking down as I saber a magnum of Moet et Chandon Brut Imperial to the beat of Ricky Martin for a group of physicians and their spouses.

My colleague, a very talented female sommelier, turns me on to Champagne and caviar scooped directly out of a gigantic tin with Lay's sour cream and onion potato chips. I am in heaven!

I am lugging six bottles of Tête de Cuvée Champagne on my shoulder through Miami International Airport. Later, I'm enjoying these bottles with my traveling companion as we sail through the Caribbean on the *Crystal Harmony*.

On the *Crystal Symphony*, I discover Mumm Cordon Rouge in the casino and promptly take up gambling. We are closing down the lounge one night, and I convince the sommelier to drink Champagne from the shoe of my exotically beautiful traveling companion. His girlfriend, the guest yoga instructor, now hates me. His boss, the beverage director, is disgusted. She lets me know it by scowling at me every time she sees me. Later I am invited to saber a bottle in the captain's quarters, where I attempt to redeem myself by giving a great show.

I am traveling alone on a research mission on the *Seabourn Legend*, a small but luxurious sailing vessel. I am being waited on hand and foot, and the men are flirting voraciously. I am trying to get through a glass of Heidsieck Monopole Blue Top, thinking that I will drink far less on this cruise than I did on the *Silver Wind*, where the exquisite Philipponnat Royale Réserve was flowing like water.

I am in my cabin on the *Silver Wind*, drinking Pol Roger Cuvée Sir Winston Churchill with my traveling companion, the sommelier, and our favorite bartender. We use the endless supply of Philopponnat as a chaser. We marvel at the moon and stars, the blackness of the sky, the mist and scent of the sea, and our temporary freedom. We get drunk. I throw my glass overboard, muttering something about glass being recyclable. Later on in the cruise, I am considering offers from a Polish drummer and a man old enough to be my grandfather, which are tempting as long as the Champagne is flowing. Fortunately morning and caffeine come along.

I am in Heather Locklear's kitchen, standing sentinel in front of the fridge while the bottles of her favorite Louis Roederer Cristal are chilling down. I have been invited to saber for her husband Richie Sambora's birthday celebration. The caterers forget the ice. It is nearly a hundred degrees out. I fight off the celebrity chef and his staff, who keep trying to put their trays of beautifully designed appetizers in the fridge. I promise them glasses of Champagne if they just let me have ten more minutes to chill my bottles. I am approached by a very warm and friendly Heather, who asks me politely if she could give my sword to Richie after my performance. Naturally I agree. Heather sends a handwritten thank-you note. My brothers, single and married, ask me to respond with their phone numbers.

I am coming home from a rough night at Aqua. I've served so many bottles of Louis Roederer Cristal to the Redford party that I am now badly Jones-ing for one. I unlock my wine fridge, take out my last bottle of 1996 Cristal, and proceed to chug it directly from the bottle, my boyfriend staring at me in disbelief.

My man and I are sitting on the beach in front of Ghirardelli Square, snuggling up and drinking our favorite, Bollinger Grand Année. We run out. He goes to his car and grabs a half bottle of Billecart-Salmon Brut Rosé, which we use as a chaser. I wonder what the poor people are doing.

I am still wondering what happened to the man who wanted to drink Champagne from my navel.

I. Introduction to Champagne & Sparkling Wine

1. Getting Comfortable with Champagne & Sparkling Wine

Welcome to *Champagne & Sparkling Wine*. In this introductory section, you'll be introduced to the world's most seductive beverage, Champagne. You will learn about its climate and soil, grape varieties, history, production methods, and styles. You will also learn about other sparkling wines from around the world, and about how to enjoy them. Then, in *Entertaining with Champagne & Sparkling Wine*, we'll review styles and types, then move into how to taste and evaluate, how to understand labels, how to shop and get the best deals, how to pair Champagne with food, and how to add zest to your parties, from small romantic affairs to formal weddings. Throughout this guide we'll raise your comfort level and confidence with Sensual Experience and Shopping Skills exercises. This will be the beginning of a beautiful and long-lasting relationship with one of the most pleasurable beverages on the planet!

The pleasures of the table are for every man, of every land, an no matter of what place in history or society; they can be part of all his other pleasures, and they last the longest, to console him when he has outlived the rest.

—Jean Anthelme Brillat-Savarin

2. Extravagant Living

Hearing, reading, or saying the word Champagne brings to mind many things, none of which are ordinary or mundane. You may have grown to expect Champagne at celebratory moments in your life—at birthdays, anniversaries, graduations, weddings, and New Year's Eve parties—and while toasting others in theirs, a race car driver as he crosses the finish line, a Skipper as he takes the winner's cup in a regatta, or even a magnificent cruise ship, christened with a bottle across its bow before it is launched on the high seas. It is easy to associate Champagne with romance, the requisite bottle chilling in a gleaming silver bucket or, in the case of James Bond, in a convenient built-in cooler located at arm's reach in the front seat of the car. Finally, Champagne is associated with the beginning of a meal, especially if in France, where it is the quintessential aperitif.

Champagne with its foaming whirls, as white as Cleopatra's pearls.

—Byron

3. What Is Le Champagne?

Champagne wines, or Champagnes, are referred to as *les Champagnes*, so *le Champagne* is the actual product itself. The name Champagne designates that the wines are produced in a strictly demarcated region. Unlike wine from other regions, where the best wines are from one varietal, one estate, and one vintage, classic Nonvintage Champagnes are a blend of different grapes from different areas and different harvests. Winemakers select and blend from various vineyard areas in the same way a perfume blender builds a perfume or a chef builds a dish. They use a base, or foundation, then round it out.

grape goddess says:

Champagne has many nicknames, including fizz, bubbly, and, one of my favorites, giggle juice.

4. What Is La Champagne?

Champagne is the name of an old province in France some 90 miles north east of Paris, where wines have been produced since Roman times. The region is referred to as la Champagne. It is the northernmost wine appellation, or controlled growing region, in France. The locals are known as *Champenois*. Champagne's region of production, established by law in 1927, spreads over 312 villages, or *crus*, and encompasses the Montagne de Reims, Vallee de la Marne, Cote des Blancs, the Coteaux de Sezanne, and the Aube. Vineyards stretch for miles along chalky slopes. The entire delimited area covers about 85,000 acres, and comprises only 2.5% of all French vineyards. Three main grape varieties are grown: Pinot Noir, Pinot Meunier, and Chardonnay.

Now That's a Bubble Bath

Ultra-feminine and lusciously curvaceous Marilyn Monroe once took a bath in 350 bottles of Champagne. Without Marilyn's bank account, but still curious, I took a bath in three bottles of Philopponnat Royale Réserve, but I had to add warm water to fill up the tub. The tepid yellow bath water did nothing for me. A spontaneous Champagne shower is much more exciting, but seeing my man drinking Champagne from my shoe warms me to the very core.

5. Five Major Vineyard Areas Make Up La Champagne

Montagne de Reims is a wide plateau gently rising and then sloping to the valleys of the Vesle and the Ardre to the north and the valley of the Marne to the south. Vines cover the flanks of the plateau, most of which are planted to Pinot Noir. Vallee de la Marne extends for 60 miles from Saacy-sur-Marne near Chateau-Thierry to Tours-sur-Marne, east of Epernay. The vineyards spread over the slopes on both sides of the river and are planted primarily to Pinot Noir and Pinot Meunier. Cote des Blancs owes its name to the predominance of Chardonnay grapes grown there. It is a steep slope stretching southwards of Epernay. Coteaux de Sezanne is an extension of the Cote des Blancs on the slopes north and south of Sezanne. This area also favors Chardonnay. Aube is the southernmost vineyard area and a highly valued source of Pinot Meunier. As with the five fingers on a hand, each digit functions alone but some tasks require all five.

My only regret in life is that I did not drink more Champagne.

—John Maynard Keynes

6. Regulatory Bored

The Comité Interprofessionnel du Vin de Champagne, or CIVC, was formed in 1942 and regulates vineyard practices, marketing, vinification methods, and maturation. Individual vineyards are graded from 50 to 100% for price. This is called the *échelle des crus*. Each year, CIVC gives a price for the vintage, and they determine when to pick. The grade given determines the price paid for the grapes. If the vineyard receives an 80% rating, the owner will receive 80% of the price determined that year. If the vineyard receives a 100% score, 100% of the price will be paid and the vineyard area is named as a *Grand Cru*. Only seventeen vineyard areas in Champagne have Grand Cru status. Many Tête de Cuvée, or top-of-the-line, Champagnes claim to use only Grand Cru fruit.

Trysting Time

Cinq à sept, or 5:00 to 7:00 P.M., is known as the trysting time for lovers in France. This is an ideal time to rendezvous with friends and sip Champagne.

7. It' Ain't the Beach, Brah

The climate of Champagne, a blend of northern continental and Atlantic influences with an annual average temperature of 51° F, couldn't be any further removed from the sun-drenched tropical islands of Hawaii, where I picked up some new slang words, such as "brah" (brother) and "broke da mouth" (delicious), while on a research mission. Due to these borderline conditions, the duration of the vine's growth cycle is stretched to the limit, resulting in a longer ripening period than you'd find in a more moderate climate. Consequently, the wines have a high sugar-to-acid ratio, subtle aromas, elegance, and finesse. Variations in altitude, humidity, angle of slope, vegetal cover ("leaves, brah"), and exposure to sun create numerous micro-climates within the region.

Sensual Experience Exercise

Micro-climates are individual pockets of weather patterns. Walk from the hot sun into the cool shade. You've just passed through two micro-climates. You're awesome!

Champagne for my true friends. True pain for my sham friends.

—Dan Berger, wine writer

8. The Dirt on France

Thirty million years ago, violent earthquakes caused the ocean floor to rise, bringing up chalk and mineral layers. Eleven million years later, another quake brought the floor up even higher, leaving what are known today as the Champagne Cliffs. Their chalk soil has a high limestone content, owing to the fossilized remains of marine life left behind when the sea receded. The deep chalky subsoil stores the heat of the sun and radiates warmth into the vine roots. Think of this as keeping your feet warm. It provides excellent drainage while preserving humidity and supplies mineral elements to the vines that you actually can taste in the final product.

Sensual Experience Exercise

Imagine a huge mountain of oyster shells baking in the hot sun, and what that would smell like. "Chalky," "slatey," and "minerally" are words often used to describe Champagne, referring to aromas and flavors found in the wine when your sensory receptors are supercharged. This may or may not work for you. The word "yummy" is fine, or you may also say, "I give this wine a smiley face."

A Monk

Upon tasting Champagne for the first time, Dom Perignon called out to his fellow monks, "Come quickly, I'm drinking stars!"

9. Cavemen with Great Skin

Soil makeup and micro-climates (remember the hot sun and the shade) determine the subtle differences between each *cru*, or village, and influence the characteristics of individual wines. The chalk subsoil extends down hundreds of feet and provides ideal cellars for storing the wines of Champagne at a constant temperature and humidity. These caves, or *crayeres*, are mostly located under the cities of Reims, Epernay, Ay, and Chalon-sur-Marne. I've observed that the men who work in these caves (all day, every day) have very few wrinkles on their dewy skin.

The effervescence of this fresh wine reveals the true brilliance of the French people.

—Voltaire

10. Tantalizing Trio

Over the centuries, three grape varieties have proven to be best suited to the soil, climate, and micro-climates of Champagne: Pinot Noir for body, strength, and fullness; Pinot Meunier for freshness, youth, and suppleness; and Chardonnay for lightness, elegance, and finesse. Pinot Meunier is considered the workhorse grape and gets little respect, but it gives young Champagne the flesh and fruit to make it that much more enjoyable right now. Need I remind anyone that the best time for Champagne is right now?

Not only does one drink Champagne, but one inhales it, one looks at it, and one swallows it.

—King Edward VII

11. What the Devil?

Did Dom Perignon invent Champagne? No. The Romans noted the possibility and the Bible mentions "wine that moveth." There is documented evidence that monks of the Abbey of St-Hilaire, in Limoux, accepted orders for sparkling wine in 1531. However the most notable developments in the production of Champagne took place in the late seventeenth century. At this time, the onset of winter prevented the wines from completing their fermentations. The process restarted as temperatures rose during the spring. The wines finished fermenting in the bottle and had a slight sparkle. Quite often a bottle exploded as natural gas pressure built up inside. These wines were called *vins du diable*, devil's wine, as there was an incomplete understanding of fermentation.

Holy Crapaud

Fine Champagne has the tiniest of bubbles. In fact, the French consider big bubbles so ugly that they call them *oeil de crapaud*, or eye of the toad.

12. More History (Yawn)—Two Guys Who Score

In the 1700s, after the coronation of Louis XIV (the king who gets the bling), the young monk Dom Pierre Perignon (the guy who spends his days drinking Champagne) was appointed cellarer at the Abbey of Hautvilliers, and Champagne began its evolution into the product we know today. This cool cat is credited with picking early, selecting the best grapes, and inventing the concept of blending. He also reintroduced the cork to northern France and used a shallow-based press to produce clear juice from black grapes. At the same time, stronger glass bottles became available. At this point, history becomes her story.

You Go Girl!

Champagne widows, the most famous of which was undoubtedly La Veuve (the widow) Clicquot, assumed responsibility for their firms after their husbands died, often expanding their holdings and sales. Madame Lily Bollinger, Madame Veuve Pommery, Madame Laurent-Perrier, Madame Olry Roederer, and others are honored to this day for their contributions to Champagne's quality and availability.

13. Honey, What Happened to the Kitchen Table?

In 1806, Miss Thang Clicquot (er, ah, Madame) invented the riddling rack. Apparently, the distressed young widow would go down at night to her kitchen table, where she had hacked holes to hold the bottles upside down, remove them, shake them to disturb the sediment, and replace them. This process is known as *remuage*. Later that century, the house of Jacquesson designed and patented the capsules that cover the cork, and both Perrier Jouet and Pommery sold the first dry, or Brut, Champagnes, though the reception was lukewarm. Brut Champagnes were a flop, so the savvy Champenois coined the phrase Extra Dry for an off-dry, slightly-sweet style, which became an overnight sensation. To this day, people still enjoy ordering dry but drinking sweet.

grape goddess says:

"vuhhvve klee koh. Repeat after me. Vuhhvve klee koh."

14. Tiny Bubbles

The four main methods of producing sparkling wine are: Charmat or Cuve Close, Transversage, Carbonation, and Méthode Champenoise. They all aim to produce a clear wine containing bubbles of carbon dioxide. Charmat/Cuve Close, invented in 1907 by Eugene Charmat, is a bulk-production method of making inexpensive sparkling wine through a natural second fermentation inside a sealed vat. In Transversage, sparkling wines undergo second fermentation in bottle and are then decanted, filtered, and re-bottled under pressure to preserve the mousse. This method is used for quarter bottles and large-sized bottles. Carbonation is the quickest and cheapest method of production, and the poorest in terms of quality. Wine is chilled in large tanks, and carbon dioxide gas is pumped into it, as in soda production. The wine is bottled under pressure.

Excellent Choice

Italy's Asti Spumante, made with the Muscat grapes using the Charmat method, is incredibly refreshing, not too dry, lighter in alcohol than French Champagne, and about $10 a bottle, making it a great picnic, brunch, or party choice.

15. Okay, Give One to the French

All Champagne is sparkling wine, but not all sparkling wine is Champagne. Méthode Champenoise, the most complex production method, is also the only method used in the Champagne region. The Champenois art begins in the vineyards with specific planting, pruning, and training methods that keep the vines low and ensure maximum sun exposure. Limited yields, constant care, and hand picking at harvest time ensure that only the finest grapes (uh huh) are selected. Okay, in this case, it really is true, because Miss Thang, the big bad boss lady, is watching, and the workers know better than to get her knickers in a twist. Méthode Champenoise is a labor-intensive, expensive process that reveals itself in the supreme quality of the final product.

FYBs

In the California sparkling wine industry, vineyard workers use "f—ing yellow boxes" to transport their delicate grapes to the winery.

16. My Little Squeeze Box

Pressing takes place at 2000 press houses scattered throughout the Champagne vineyards, many of which are traditional (really old) 4000-kilo capacity Coquard presses. Wine presses are placed in the vineyards during harvest to allow the wine-maker to press the red grapes immediately without extracting any of the color. Even the amount of juice they can press out is regulated here; it is limited to 26.4 gallons for every 330 lbs of grapes, equivalent to 100 liters of Champagne for every 160 kilograms of grapes.

Wine Geek Alert!

The first pressing is called the cuvée and the second pressing the taille. Since the 1993 Le Colibri revision of the 1987 Quality Charter, only the juice from the cuvée and taille can be used to make Champagne wines.

Champagne is the only wine that leaves a woman beautiful after drinking it.

—Madame du Pompadour

17. Finishing School

In the cellars, the freshly pressed, or squeezed, grape juice goes into stainless-steel tanks, vats, or neutral casks for the first fermentation, where yeasts feed on grape sugars, giving off the by-products alcohol and carbon dioxide gas. After a few weeks, the juice is transformed into very dry and highly acidic still wine. The wine may then undergo malolactic fermentation (wine geek alert!), a biochemical process that converts hard malic acid to soft lactic acid. By the end of winter, the still wines become clear, *vins clairs*, as their slimy sediment drops out, and each one is assessed for its specific character, aroma, acidity, and body.

Tip:

Do not—I repeat, do not—taste tank samples in Champagne, unless you'd like to expose every raw nerve ending in your mouth. These viciously acidic wines strip the enamel right off the teeth.

Whoa!

According to scientist Bill Lembeck, there are 49 million bubbles in a bottle of Champagne.

18. What a Schnoz

Assemblage, or assembling the blend, is at the core of the Champenois art. A characteristic and consistent style is achieved by marrying wines from as many as seventy base wines from individual *crus*, grape varieties, and vintages. Those who perform the assemblage are known as "noses," like their counterparts in perfume-blending houses. Consistent, or signature house style is one of the reasons for Champagne's long lasting success. A bottle of Mumm Cordon Rouge will most likely taste the same anywhere on planet Earth, and over the span of a lifetime. Unlike many of the wines from Burgundy or the cult wines from Napa Valley, the price for Champagne is very fair for the quality, and disappointments are rare.

Attention Grabber

The reason servers in French bistros make a big show of opening and serving Champagne, raising the bottle high in the air between pours, is to attract the attention of everyone in the dining room, who all look over and think, "I want what they're having."

19. Where the Party At

When *assemblage*, assembling the blend, is complete, the wine undergoes a final racking. It is transferred into a fresh, clean tank and then the party begins. *Liqueur de tirage*, a mixture of still Champagne, sugar, and selected yeasts, is added. The amount of sugar added depends on the degree of effervescence desired and the amount of natural sugar in the wine. The wines are bottled and crown capped with a small plastic pot below the metal cap to catch the sediment produced by the second fermentation. These crown caps are just like those found on bottled beer and soda. Bottles are stacked *sur lattes*, on their sides, in dark, cool, chalky cellars. Yeasts feed leisurely on the new sugar supply, giving off carbon dioxide again as a by-product, but this time the gas has nowhere to go. It is captured inside the bottle over a period of ten days to three months. This captured gas is called *prise de mousse*, and the Champenois have been learning to control it for the past three centuries.

Champagne is the one thing that gives me zest when I feel tired.

—Brigette Bardot

20. Shake, Rattle, and Roll

After the second fermentation, bottles are moved to *pupitres*, wooden racks, or to *gyropalettes*, big wire cages full of bottles that move mechanically, for riddling, or *remuage*, the method invented by Madame Clicquot, which involves shaking and twisting the bottles to loosen the expired yeast sediment and encourage it to move down to the neck. By hand, this takes eight weeks. By machine, it takes eight days. The *gyropalette*, adapted from the Spanish *girasol*, is in common use by the Champagne industry today for all but the high end luxury cuvées.

Labor Intensive

Luxury cuvées from some of the top California sparkling wine producers, including Schramsberg and Iron Horse, are riddled by hand.

21. Slip and Slide

Autolysis is the aging period that follows riddling. Nonvintage Champagne must age for fifteen months, and vintage Champagne must age for at least three years. The longer the Champagne is aged on its lees (not on your kitchen shelf), the better it becomes, as this slimy, sludgy sediment broadens the scope of flavors and complexity of the wine. If you hear or read a Champagne review and the word "autolytic" is used, this refers to that yeasty, tangy character imparted to the wine from that slimy goo.

The priest has just baptized you a Christian with water, and I baptize you a Frenchman, darling child, with a dewdrop of Champagne on your lips.

—Paul Claudel

22. Shooting Up

Degorgement, or disgorging, is the removal of the sediment that has collected in the little plastic tub under the crown cap during aging. Bottlenecks are immersed in a shallow bath of freezing brine, which solidifies the mass into the cap. Next, bottles are turned upright and uncapped, and the sediment plug shoots out, riding on built-up pressure. Finally, bottles are topped up with *liqueur d'expedition,* made up of still Champagne, a dose of sugar, and even a drop of brandy (though it is rarely admitted). The amount of sugar added here determines how dry the final product will be.

> *If the aunt of the Vicar has never touched liquor, watch out when she finds the Champagne.*

> —Rudyard Kipling

23. How Sweet It Was

The amount of sugar added, or dosage, determines whether the Champagne will be dry (Brut), a bit sweeter (Extra Dry), or very sweet (Demi-sec). Until 1850, all Champagne was sweet. A few houses release zero-dosage Champagnes labeled as Extra Brut, or Brut Nature. CIVC regulations allow Extra Brut 3–6 grams/liter and Brut Nature 0–3 grams/liter. Bottles are then corked, muzzled with a protective wire cage, labeled, and shipped off to every corner of the globe.

The Cat's Meow

Why drink Champagne? The wire muzzles make great cat toys.

24. Styled and Dialed

Nonvintage (nv) is the signature or house style. Consistently and widely available, it generally retails at $25–40. Vintage is from a single harvest, or year, and generally retails from $40 to 60. Tête de Cuvée is the top-of-the-line luxury cuvée, with a retail range of $80–150. Blanc de Blancs is made from white grapes only, Chardonnay. Blanc de Noirs is made from black, or red, grapes only, Pinot Noir and Pinot Meunier. Rosé is unusual in that the law here allows either *saignée*, tapping the tank to drain off pink-colored juice before it has taken on too much color from contact with grape skins, or the addition of still red wine, known as Bouzy rouge. Very few regions in the world allow the addition of red wine to a white wine to make a pink wine.

grape goddess says:

"Blah-nn-kk duh blah-nn-kk, blah-nn-kk duh nw-are

Repeat after me.

Blah-nn-kk duh blah-nn-kk, blah-nn-kk duh nw-are."

25. Bottle Sizes

Split—187ml
Half-Bottle—375ml
Bottle—750 ml
Magnum—1.5 L (2 bottles)
Jeroboam—3.0L (4 bottles)
Methuselah—8 bottles
Salmanazar—12 bottles
Balthazar—16 bottles
Nebuchadnezzar—20 bottles

Tip:

A standard 750 ml bottle is usually just about right for two.

May you have the hindsight to know where you've been, the foresight to know where you're going, and the insight to know when you're going too far.

—Champagne toast

26. More Giggle Juice

Besides Champagne, France also produces Limoux from the Southwest, Saumur from the Loire Valley, Cremant d'Alsace, and Cremant de Bourgogne sparkling wines. Cava, one of the most famous sparkling wines in the world, comes from Spain. Asti Spumante, Moscato d'Asti, and the Méthode Champenoise styles of Lombardy all come from Italy. Germany has Sekt, Israel has Blanc de Blancs, Australia has Sparkling Shiraz, and the USA produces sparkling wine of all quality levels both in California and New York State.

grape goddess recommends:

Korbel Chardonnay Champagne, California, $11, Domaine Laurens Blanquette de Limoux, France, $14, Iron Horse Blanc de Blancs Sonoma County Green Valley, California, $28, Schramsberg Reserve, California, $65, Montenisa Brut, Franciacorta, Italy, $32, Nicolas Feuillatte Blanc de Blancs Champagne, France, $45, Bollinger Grand Année Brut Champagne, France, $90, or *Philipponnat Clos de Goisses Champagne, France, $130.*

27. I'm Cool Like That. I'm Chill Like That

Store bubblies in a cool, dark place away from heat, light, vibrations, and severe temperature variations. Champagnes are ready to drink upon release and, for the most part, do not improve with age. Bottles do not need to be stored on their sides. Before serving, chill the wine well, but do not freeze it. Place the bottle in a bucket filled with ice and just enough water to make a thick soup. Let it sit there for twenty minutes. Always keep a chilled bottle in the fridge, because you never know. Besides, giggle juice goes with everything. Don't wait for an occasion. Make one.

White with light clothes, Red with dark clothes, Champagne without clothes, and beer with someone ugly.

—Sommelier's toast

28. A Maiden's Sigh

The pressure in a bottle of Champagne is equivalent to that of a London double-decker bus tire, or about 90 pounds per square inch. When opening, the goal is to hear the sound of a satisfied maiden's sigh, or a baby's fart, not the bellowing ballpark hot dog and garlic fries beer belly belch.

Sensual Experience Exercise

Slant the bottle at a 45-degree angle away from guests and any others in the vicinity. Placing a thumb on the cork to hold it down, untwist and loosen the wire muzzle. Grasp the cork firmly, twist the bottle slowly and let the pressure help ease out the cork while maintaining greater pressure on it. Holding the bottle at an angle is best. Why? Well, would you like the gas to come out as liquid or vapor?

Tip:

Don't open a bottle of Champagne or sparkling wine unless it has been chilled on ice for 20 minutes, in the freezer for 15 minutes, or in the refrigerator for 45 minutes. Warm bottles or those that have been jostled around are not safe to open.

29. Top-Shelf Service

Drinking vessels for Champagne really depend on the situation. Anything from a navel to a lady's stiletto slipper is fine, and sometimes doing Champagne shooters out of the bottle is the only option. However, if you are having a classy affair, serve sparkling wine in tall flutes or tulip glasses at a temperature of 42–47°F or to your liking. Pour a small amount into the glass, allow the bubbles to liquefy, then top up to about half full. Tall, narrow flutes keep the tiny bubbles flowing, like oil gurgling up from a well. The wider, shallow coupe style of glass allows gas to dissipate quickly, showcasing the taste of the base wine.

Sensual Experience Exercise

When no one is looking, take a sip of Champagne straight from the bottle.

Tip:

Leftovers? What are those? If you do have them, Champagne stoppers are the only way to fully protect the gas. Interestingly, some Champagnes taste fuller and mellower the next day.

30. Congratulations!

How do you feel? Thirsty? Up for an adventure? Excellent. Go forth into the world of giggle juice and show them your stuff. After checking your progress with the following review quiz (you'll find the answer key on page 69), continue on to *Entertaining with Champagne & Sparkling Wine.*

> *Shoot for the moon. Even if you miss, you'll land among the stars.*

—Les Brown

INTRODUCTION TO CHAMPAGNE & SPARKLING WINE

Check Your Success Quiz

1. La Champagne is

    a. the wine produced in a strictly demarcated region.

    b. made from a blend of different grapes from different areas and different harvests.

    c. the name of an old province in France.

    d. made from a blend of different grapes from the same harvest.

2. The entire delimited vineyard area of Champagne covers about

    a. 85,000 acres.

    b. 185,000 acres.

    c. 8,500 acres.

    d. 885,000 acres.

3. The climate of Champagne has an annual average temperature of

    a. 31°F.

    b. 41°F.

    c. 51°F.

    d. 61°F.

4. Micro-climate is

    a. the ambient temperature at root level.

    b. an individual pocket of a weather pattern.

    c. figured by combining average temperature and average rainfall.

    d. the angle of the sun.

5. Who or what invented Champagne?

    a. Madame Veuve Clicquot

    b. Nature

    c. Monks of the Abbey of St. Hilaire

    d. Dom Perignon

6. In Champagne labeling, Extra Dry refers to

    a. a slightly sweet style.

    b. a dry style.

    c. a bone dry, austere style.

    d. a type of vermouth.

7. Press houses in Champagne are

    a. adjacent to the main headquarters of the winery.

    b. strategically located on hilltops.

    c. open to visitors .

    d. scattered throughout the vineyards.

8. Big bubbles are referred to by the French as

    a. *amusant.*

    b. *oeil de perdrix.*

    c. *oeil de crapaud.*

    d. *assemblage.*

9. Bouzy Rouge is

    a. a rich, fruity red available in every bistro in the area.

    b. a still red wine added to white base wine to make pink Champagne.

    c. the local nickname for the red cheeks caused from over-indulgence.

    d. a *Grand Cru* village known for Pinot Noir.

10. The best way to chill a standard 750 ml bottle of Champagne is to

    a. place in the refrigerator for 45 minutes.

b. place in the refrigerator for 30 minutes.

c. place in the freezer for 45 minutes.

d. place in the freezer for 30 minutes.

II. Entertaining with Champagne & Sparkling Wine

1. Taking It to the Next Level

Welcome to *Entertaining with Champagne & Sparkling Wine*. The focus of this section is to get you comfortable with all aspects of entertaining with bubbly, so we'll first review styles and types, then move into how to taste and evaluate Champagne, how to understand labels, how to shop and get the best deals, how to pair Champagne with food, and how to add zest to your parties, from small romantic affairs to formal weddings. Along the way, we'll do plenty of Sensual Experience and Shopping Skills exercises to hone your skills and turn you into an expert. Get ready to snuggle up even closer to one of the most pleasurable beverages in the solar system.

I like restraint, if it doesn't go too far.

—Mae West

2. Cool Review

Champagne is the northernmost wine appellation, or controlled growing region, in France. The Atlantic-influenced climate is cold and wet, and the area is prone to frost. Porous chalk soils store and dispense solar heat and humidity, encourage the vine to produce grapes with high acidity, and give finesse and lightness to the wine. Champagne is a blended wine, made up of wines from across the region from a blend of the grapes Chardonnay, Pinot Noir, and/or Pinot Meunier. What is so truly amazing is that the best of these golden, glistening, spirited nectars come from the most inhospitable environments.

The moment one gives close attention to anything, even a blade of grass, it becomes a mysterious, awesome, indescribably magnificent world in itself.

—Henry Miller

3. Remember This

All Champagne is sparkling wine, but not all sparkling wine is Champagne. Bubblies are produced all over planet Earth in the rest of France, Italy, Germany, Austria, Spain, Israel, South Africa, Australia, South America, and North America. The best of these are made by the classic Méthode Champenoise, and the classic grapes: Chardonnay, Pinot Noir, and/or Pinot Meunier.

Tip:

Looking for fun fizz? Cava from Spain, Prosecco from Italy, sparkling Shiraz from Australia, sparkling Riesling from New York State, and sparkling ice wine from Ontario, Canada, may tickle your fancy. Some of America's most highly rated sparkling wines are from New York State, but don't tell that to a Californian!

4. Three Tiers

Champagne is easily categorized into three tiers. The first is Nonvintage, or nv, a blend of wines from the current year's harvest with reserve wines of varying ages obtained from previous harvests. The second is Vintage, blended from wines of a single year's harvest. No reserve wines are used, and the year of the crop appears on the label. Third is Prestige or Luxury Cuvée, a superior blend of the rarest wines representing the best the house has to offer. In the house of Moet et Chandon, for example, level one is their Brut nv, about $30. Level two is their Vintage Brut, about $60. And their Luxury Cuvée, Dom Perignon, is about $90. Remember this as the 30/60/90 principle.

The Power of Marketing

You'd be surprised if you tasted these three blind. You might not choose Dom Perignon as your favorite if you went by taste alone. However, by looking at the bottles, chances are you would choose the Prestige Cuvée. Hugh Davies of Schramsberg, in Napa Valley, proves this point by including his Schramsberg Reserve, a $65 California sparkling wine, in a blind tasting alongside Luxury Cuvée Champagnes at $100 and up, including Dom Perignon, Cristal, La Grande Dame, Perrier-Jouet Fleur de Champagne, and Krug. His wine consistently takes third or fourth place, and you'd never believe which one consistently ranks last!

A connoisseur is curious about new and even unheard-of brands and labels. Geeks and snobs buy all their wines by the label and what they have heard about them.

—Randal Caparoso, winemaker and writer

5. In the Pink

Despite the general perception, Brut Rosé is not for ladies only, although the very thought of it brings mouthwatering visions of decadence and frolic to mind. Brut Rosé is actually the weightiest and richest of Champagne styles, is made in all three tiers, and often is the best Champagne to serve with the main course. Rosé Champagne and lamb, for example, is an incredible match.

Sensual Experience Exercise

Serve a Blanc de Noirs or Rosé to your partner, but ask them to close their eyes before taking the first sip. Then ask them to describe it to you. Finally, ask them to open their eyes and look at the color. They just might be pleasantly surprised!

Tip:

Pink bubbly has gotten a bad rap in areas outside of Champagne. Many think its pink color makes it a less serious wine and can't understand why it is dry and expensive. This is not bubbling White Zinfandel! Rosé Champagne is generally a dry (Brut) style and gets its pink, salmon, or even copper color from the addition of red wine from Pinot Noir, or from skin contact with Pinot Noir skins. This extra process adds to the cost, but for your extra investment you get a bubbly that has the bonus berry flavors of Pinot Noir.

6. How Sweet it Is

The amount of sugar added, or dosage, determines whether the Champagne will be dry or Brut, a bit sweeter (Extra Dry), or very sweet (Demi-sec). You will most often encounter Brut and Extra Dry styles. On occasion you may come across a Demi-sec, or dessert style Champagne, such as Piper-Heidsieck Cuvée Sublime. The California sparkling wine Schramsberg Crémant is a Demi-sec style.

Zero-dosage Champagne is not very popular and thus is hard to find. It may be labeled as Extra Brut, or Brut Nature. Extra Brut has 3–6 grams/liter of sugar and Brut Nature 0–3 grams/liter. Laurent Perrier Ultra Brut is a good example of an Extra Brut.

Extra Dry Champagnes are the best selling in America, driven by the hugely successful Moet et Chandon White Star. Minis, the 187-ml brightly-colored single-serving bottles so popular in bars and night clubs, are in the Extra Dry category as well. They include the striking cobalt-blue Pommery Pops, the hot-pink Pommery Pops Rosé, and the fire-engine-red Piper Heidsieck Baby. The California sparkling wine Iron Horse Russian Cuvée is an Extra Dry style.

7. Champagne House Styles

Over the years, the Champagne houses have developed their own signature styles. Most major houses fall into one of three categories: light, medium, or full-bodied.

If you prefer a light and delicate style, choose
Ayala, Billecart Salmon, Jacquesson, Jacques Selosses, Lanson, Mumm, Nicolas Feuillatte, Perrier Jouet, or Salon.

For a medium-bodied style, try
Bruno Paillard, Charles Heidsieck, Deutz, Dom Ruinart, Henriot, Laurent Perrier, Moet et Chandon, Philipponnat, Pommery, Pol Roger, or Veuve Clicquot.

For a full-bodied style, select
Bollinger, Delbeck, Gosset, Krug, or Louis Roederer.

If a house makes a sparkling wine in another area—say, California or Australia—and the same brand name is used on the bottle, chances are that this wine will also represent the house style. This is the case with Champagne Louis Roederer, a house known for its big, rich, decadent style, and their California sparkling wines, including Roederer L'Ermitage.

I am easily satisfied with the best.

—Sir Winston Churchill

8. Tasting

Tasting bubbly is as easy as picking up your flute, looking at the color, feeling your nose prickle as tiny CO_2 bubbles migrate upwards, listening to that wonderful fizzing sound, and, finally, taking a small sip. That's all there is to it. Bubbly doesn't need to be swirled in the glass or swished around on the palate. The fizz does the work for you.

Sensual Experience Exercise

Take out your notebook and write a few descriptors next to the brand name and other label information you've entered.

Getting in the Mood

Picking up a flute of Champagne and listening to its steady stream of bubbles is as mesmerizing as listening to the sound of the sea in a conch shell. By the way, conch has proven in my research to be a powerful and fast-acting aphrodisiac, especially for men.

9. Evaluating

Did you like what you tasted? Why? Was there something particular about it, or was it just really yummy? The point of keeping a log of your tastings is so that you will remember what you liked. You may also see yourself leaning towards a particular type or style, or even towards a specific brand. Champagne brands are extremely consistent. Say you discover that, like me, that you favor Bollinger. Whether enjoying the stimulating Bollinger Special Cuvée, the seductive Bollinger Grand Année, or the sleek, powerful Ferrari of Champagne, Bollinger RD, two, four, six, or even eight years from now, chances are that you'll have the same experience with the brand. It becomes like an old, reliable friend.

Trustworthy

The beauty of Champagne's consistency is that anywhere you are in the world, you'll know what to expect when you see a familiar *marque*, or brand name. This comes in handy at resorts, which often have high mark-ups on wine. By ordering a familiar brand of Champagne, at least you know what you are getting for your money.

10. Designer Label

Look for the name "Champagne" standing alone and the words "Product of France" on the label. The brand name, or *marque*, is important, as is the degree of sweetness or dryness (Brut, Extra Dry, and so on). You'll also fine the name of a town, such as Reims, where the wine was made, and the alcohol content. Keep in mind that most Champagnes are blended from vineyards all across the Champagne region, so the town on the label simply refers to the location of offices and caves. Also check for a reference to grape type, Blanc de Blancs, Blanc de Noirs, and the vintage year if it is in that category. You'll rarely see the words Premier Cru or Grand Cru on a Champagne label, as you might with Burgundy, for example. You may not even see the top-rated vineyard's name. Again, this goes back to Champagne reflecting the house style, its brand identity rather than the grape type or vineyard.

For Wine Geeks Only

Look closely and you'll also find a registration number preceded by two initials: N.M. for Negociant Manipulant, a Champagne firm's wine, R.M. for Recoltant Manipulant, a grower's wine, or C.M. for Cooperative de Manipulation, a cooperative's wine.

11. Shopping for and finding the Best Deals

Deals abound in bubbly in all categories, including the pinnacle product, Luxury Cuvée Champagne. Rule Number 1: comparison shop. Rule Number 2: comparison shop. Rule Number 3: need I say more? Say you'd like to pick up a case of the Spanish sparkling Cava for a party and a bottle of the ultra-luxurious Louis Roederer Cristal as a gift for someone (or something) special.

Shopping Skills Exercise

If you have access to a computer, go first to a search engine and type in Cava. Check a few links and do some research on the various brands and prices. Now, go to *wine-searcher.com* and type in the brand of Cava that looked interesting and see what prices come up. Next, type in Louis Roederer Cristal and get the price spread. Now, head to the nearest discounter (or go to your local merchant if he or she is flexible). Bring a printout of the lowest prices you found and ask them to meet that price. Use your leverage. Remind them that you are not just cherry picking by asking for a discounted bottle of Louis Roederer Cristal, but that are also buying a case of the Cava. If they won't budge, and you have time, go elsewhere.

12. Sparkling Specialty Retailers

Don't pay full pop unless you have no other alternative. The best deals are generally found at close out or liquidator shops, at a wine merchant specializing in and selling a high volume of bubbly, and, occasionally, at the large chains on special promotions.

Sherry-Lehmann is a well-respected merchant in Manhattan and is one of the top Champagne retailers in America. Visit www.sherry-lehmann.com. *D&M*, a specialty merchant in San Francisco, has unbeatable prices, selection, and even a Champagne Club. Visit www.dandm.com. *Mollie Stones*, a Bay Area high-end grocer chain, has their very own "Dr. Champagne", Mr. Jerry Horn, the wine buyer in their Greenbrae location (www.molliestones.com). Scan the ads at your local grocers, drug, and warehouse outlets for discounted prices. Buy by the case whenever you find a great deal.

Champagne Society

D&M has a Champagne club where they send you a few bottles each month. In this case, because D&M is a Champagne specialty store, not some questionable operation, you can bank on these bubblies to delight, excite, and satisfy you.

13. What to Buy in Champagne

grape goddess recommends:

Nonvintage
Charles Heidsieck Brut Reserve, $30
Henriot Millesieme Brut, $35
Louis Roederer Brut Premier, $45
Nicolas Feuillatte Blanc de Blancs, Premier Cru de Chardonnay, $45

Vintage
Bollinger Grand Année Brut, $90
Duetz Vintage Brut Rosé, $46
Moet et Chandon Vintage Brut Rosé, $50
Veuve Clicquot Gold Label Vintage Reserve Brut, $50

Luxury Cuvée
Bruno Paillard "Nec Plus Ultra" NPU Brut, $150
Gosset Celebris, $130
Pol Roger Cuvée Sir Winston Churchill, $170
Pommery Cuvée Louise, $100
Philipponnat Clos de Goisses, $130

Kosher
Laurent-Perrier Kosher Brut, $52

All prices are suggested retail.

Why do I drink Champagne for breakfast? Doesn't everyone?

—Noel Coward

14. What to Buy in Sparkling Wine

grape goddess recommends:

Montenisa Brut, Franciacorta, Italy, $32
Bellavista Grand Cuvée Brut, Franciacorta, Italy, $36
Gloria Ferrer Royal Cuvée Brut, Carneros, California, $18
Iron Horse Blanc de Blancs Sonoma County Green Valley, California, $28
Schramsberg Blanc de Noirs, California, $24
Schramsberg Reserve, California, $65
Segura Viudas Brut Cava Reserva Heredad, Penedes, Spain, $17
Wolffer Estate Brut Rosé, Long Island, New York, $18
Yarden Blanc de Blancs, Golan Heights, Israel, $20

All prices are suggested retail.

grape goddess says:

Aside from the price, one of the biggest differences between sparkling wine and Champagne is that sparkling wines tend to lack that honeyed, brioche-like autolytic character (wine geek alert!).

15. Cool Deals in Bubbly

grape goddess recommends:

Domaine Laurens Blanquette de Limoux, France, $14
Korbel Chardonnay Champagne, California, $11
Rotari Blanc de Noirs Brut, Metodo Classico, Trentino-Alto-Adige, Italy, $8
Segura Viudas Aria Brut, Cava, Penedes, Spain, $9

All prices are suggested retail.

Shopping Skills Exercise

Take a notepad and jot down a few of the brands you come across in a chain or warehouse discount store, and their prices. Buy two or three different bottles, adding a few tasting notes to your notepad once you've tried them. If your budget allows, go back and pick up a case of your favorite while it is still on sale. This way, you'll have something on hand that you've personally selected by trial and error!

To a wine lover, an inexpensive wine can be a great buy. To a wine snob, it's never more than "cheap."

—Randal Caparoso, winemaker and writer

16. So Good, So Right

Bubbly has an uncanny ability to enrich one's life well beyond the occasional wedding, romantic evening, or Sunday brunch, where its character is sometimes thankfully masked by orange juice in the popular mimosa. It is a shoo-in at the beginning of the meal. In France, it is far more common to kick off a meal with a glass of Champagne than a martini or some other strong cocktail. Bubbly is easy to pair with a multitude of appetizers, entrees, and desserts. Believe it or not, olives, tortilla chips, toasted almonds, Kumamoto oysters, Caesar salad with cracked black peppercorns, monk fish, butter-poached Maine lobster, sausage and mushroom pizza, tandoori chicken, crispy duck, roast turkey, roasted pork loin, lamb chops, crème brulée, and petit fours all pair well with giggle juice. We'll explore this further in segment 17.

Alcohol is the king of potables and carries to the nth degree the excitation of our palates.

—Jean Anthelme Brillat-Savarin

17. Styled and Dialed for Starters

Here are a few combinations that work well for cocktail receptions and with appetizers:

Light/Brut/Blanc de Blancs/Luxury Cuvée

Kumamoto oysters, butter-poached Maine lobster

Medium/Brut/Nonvintage

Olives, Caesar salad with cracked black peppercorns

Light/Extra Dry/Nonvintage

Tortilla chips, toasted almonds
Smoked salmon with crème fraîche

The Four Variables

Light/medium/full
Brut/Extra Dry/Demi-sec
Blanc de Blancs/Blanc de Noirs/Rosé
Nonvintage/Vintage/Luxury Cuvée

Are you getting hungry?

18. Main Course and Dessert

Here are a few combinations that work well for the main course and one for dessert:

Medium/Blanc de Noirs or Rosé/Nonvintage

Sausage and mushroom pizza, tandoori chicken

Full/Brut/Vintage

Roast turkey, roasted pork loin

Full/Brut/Rosé

Lamb chops, crispy duck

Medium/Demi-sec/Nonvintage

Crème brulée, petit fours

The Four Variables

Light/medium/full
Brut/Extra Dry/Demi-sec
Blanc de Blancs/Blanc de Noirs/Rosé
Nonvintage/Vintage/Luxury Cuvée

19. Paradigm

Entire meals are sometimes paired with a sparkling wine at every course. This is very common in the region of origin. For example, in Champagne, your each and every course will be paired with bubbles, starting with the lightest, driest, and crispest, building up to the fullest and richest, and capping off with a Demi-sec style with dessert, as demonstrated in segments 17 and 18. Unless your crowd is ultra-serious and focused, do offer a red wine with the entrée. I spent several days in on a research mission in Bordeaux dreaming of Champagne, and when I got to Champagne, I was longing for a glass of Bordeaux.

I drink Champagne when I'm happy and when I'm sad. Sometimes I drink it when I'm alone. When I have company, I consider it obligatory. I trifle with it if I'm not hungry, and drink it when I am. Otherwise I never touch it—unless I'm thirsty.

—Madame Lily Bollinger

20. Opening Act

Remember, the pressure in a bottle of Champagne is equivalent to that of a London double-decker bus tire, about 90 pounds per square inch. Chilling reduces pressure, making the bottles safer to open.

Sensual Experience Exercise

Repeat this exercise from Section I. You can never have too much practice.

Slant the bottle at a 45-degree angle away from guests and any others in the vicinity. Placing a thumb on the cork to hold it down, untwist and loosen the wire muzzle. Grasp the cork firmly, twist the bottle slowly, and let the pressure help ease out the cork while maintaining greater pressure on it. Holding the bottle at an angle is best. Why? Well, would you like the gas to come out as liquid or vapor?

Tip:

When facing a tough cork that won't budge, use a rubber dish glove to get a better grip.

Unbidden, more than one older Frenchman has advised me that a Champagne bottle, correctly opened, should make a sound no greater than that of a contented woman's sigh. French men are French men after all.

—Karen MacNeil, wine author and educator

21. Striking

In times of triumph, Napoleon's gallant soldiers opened Champagne with a strong blow from their swords. Today top sommeliers and bubbly experts continue this dramatic tradition. Men tend to experience shortness of breath and increased heart rate when they see grape goddess wielding her sword at weddings, business openings, corporate events, and private parties:

She steps forward in a black evening gown sliced thigh-high, her faced framed by cool black shades, her chestnut mane sweeping across her milky shoulders. She dons a pair of python-patterned opera gloves. She draws the black-handled saber, inhales, and then lifts the Champagne skyward. A few quick strokes of the blade sever the neck and cork from the bottle, and they sail serenely away.

—Jonathan L. Wright, *Reno Gazette-Journal*, 4/13/2004

Tip:

Don't try this at home.

22. Smooth Operator

Serve sparkling wines in tall flute or tulip glasses, at a temperature of 42–47°F or at the temperature you prefer. Pour a small amount into a glass, let the bubbles settle, then top up to a little over half full, or more, depending on your personal preference. Keep topping up frequently with small pours. This keeps things fresh and cool.

Sensual Experience Exercise

Try grasping the bottom of the bottle, or place your hand on the back label to pour. Walk with the bottle over to a mirror and observe yourself holding the bottle this way. Now, set it down and grab it by the neck as if it were a beer. Which do you think looks better?

23. A "Shoe In"

As mentioned earlier, drinking vessels for Champagne really depend on the situation. Anything from a navel to a lady's stiletto slipper is fine, and sometimes doing Champagne shooters out of the bottle is the only option. For a classy affair, though, serve sparkling wine in tall flutes or tulip glasses. The wider, shallow coupe glass allows gas to dissipate quickly, showcasing the taste of the base wine. This also happens when using a regular wine glass.

I have more Champagne glasses in my house than I have pots and pans.

—Tina Turner

24. L'il Bit

Riedel, the hot ticket at the upper end of wine glassware, makes a giant tulip-shaped glass that holds about 10 ounces, or a double serving of bubbly. I am not personally a fan of this, as I tend prefer my bubbly cold and with lots of fizz. However, what matters most is what works for you. In Champagne bars, delicate little flutes that hold about 3 ounces are the standard.

grape goddess says:

As with all wines, glassware is the accessory, the scarf or tie to the black dress or suit. The best glass won't improve an ordinary wine, and a spectacular wine will be spectacular even in a Dixie cup.

May you live as long as you like, and have all you like as long as you live.

—Champagne toast

25. Toasting Tips

Here are a few pointers on making brilliant toasts when you're called to task. Do your homework. Mentally prepare what you're going to say or, better yet, write it down and practice it ahead of time. A good toast only seems spontaneous. Make sure everyone has a glass with which to toast. Stand and face the person or people you're toasting. As you're speaking, make eye contact with them and speak in a confident tone. Raise your glass to the toastees or, if close enough, clink glasses together, and then take a sip together. Keep your toast to a maximum length of ninety seconds. More than this is too much.

Cheers! Wen Lie! A Votre Santé! Prosit! Yasas! Kanpai! Salud!

—Champagne toasts

26. Intimate Affair

Start a fire, rekindle it, or celebrate it with the help of sparkling wine or Champagne.

Sensual Experience Exercise

Set the stage with candlelight and soft music, then open and serve two glasses, pouring in only enough to fill them halfway. Now, make a toast, looking deep into your partner's eyes, but before clinking glasses, intertwine arms, wrapping them around each other's until you are back in clinking position. Now, clink, then slowly unwrap, keeping direct eye contact, and then, once your arms are free, take a sip.

Nibble and Sip

Keeping the glasses lightly filled gives both of you frequent opportunities to get closer while topping up. Do nibble on olives, such as kalamatas or lucques, nuts, such as almonds or pistachios, and other light snacks while sipping. Wine consumed on an empty stomach is a no-no. With bubbly, this is even more important, as the CO_2 bubbles carry the alcohol immediately and directly into the bloodstream.

Here's to love, the only fire against which there is no insurance.

—Champagne toast

27. Fun and Festive Parties

Champagne theme parties create memories that last a lifetime. Set a Parisian stage, complete with "La Vie en Rose," cabaret dancers (live or on video) and plenty of bubbly all around. Or have a "Roaring Twenties" party, asking guests to come in period attire. For large crowds, consider purchasing those plastic flutes made up of two parts that snap together. With plastic flutes, cleanup is a breeze, and there is no need to worry about broken glass. Do keep the giggle juice well chilled.

Champagne, with all its amber hue, its sparkle, and its perfume, arouses the senses and produces a cheerfulness which flashes through the company like a spark of electricity.

—Jean Anthelme Brillat-Savarin

28. How Much to Serve

For a Champagne aperitif at cocktail hour, allow one bottle for every three or four guests. When served at a meal, count on one bottle for every two or three people. For an intimate affair, a bottle is just right. For festive gatherings, have one bottle for every two guests. For the traditional toast to the bride, one bottle will serve five to seven guests.

Be a generous host at your large gathering. Buy more bubbly than you think you'll need. It is always best to overestimate. Just chill in an ice bath as needed, but remember to pull extra bottles out before their labels are ruined or slip off.

My heart is as full as my glass, when I drink to you, old friend.

—Champagne toast

29. Main Event

Big events call for a wider selection of beverages. Your guests may like a choice of white or red wine, and if this is a wedding or graduation, choose a moderately-priced California or Spanish sparkling wine for the Champagne toast. Weather is also a factor. Plan on serving more chilled whites in warmer weather and more reds if the sun is hiding behind the clouds on the big day. Always provide plenty of water and non-alcoholic beverages.

Here is what top romance novelist Jackie Collins envisions for her dream Valentine's Day dinner:

> *It would be in a private bungalow in Kona, Hawaii. We'd sit on the terrace, overlooking a lagoon stocked with exotic tropical fish, and drink Champagne and eat peaches, lobster and garlic mashed potatoes, and strawberries and cream.*

30. Congratulations!

You've done it! You're a sparkling wine pro. After checking your progress with the following review quiz (for which you'll find the answer key on page 69), go out and show them your razzle-dazzle. Do your homework, negotiate firmly, and chart your course for the big event a bit in advance, and you'll have them walking on cloud nine. If you'd like to brush up on your wine basics, check out *Wine*, part of the *grape goddess guides to good living* series.

grape goddess says:

May the sensual pleasures of Champagne & Sparkling Wines enrich your daily life and, on occasion, set your wild side free.

ENTERTAINING WITH CHAMPAGNE & SPARKLING WINE

Check Your Success Quiz

1. The 30/60/90 principle refers to

    a. required temperature spreads across the growing season.

    b. Champagne press house rules.

    c. Champagne price tiers.

    d. aging and dosage.

2. The richest style of Champagne is

    a. Rosé.

    b. Luxury Cuvée.

    c. Vintage.

    d. Vintage Reserve.

3. Which of the following refers to a slightly sweet style of Champagne?

    a. Brut Nature

    b. Demi-sec

    c. Spumante

    d. Extra Dry

4. The house style for Champagne Ayala is

    a. full bodied.

    b. light bodied.

    c. Blanc de Blancs.

    d. medium bodied.

5. Which of the following is mandatory on a Champagne label?

    a. Vintage year

b. Reference to grape type

c. Premier and Grand Cru vineyard information

d. Name of the town where the wine was made

6. Which of the following is the best pairing with Rosé Champagne or Blanc de Noirs sparkling wine?

a. Caesar salad

b. Tandoori chicken

c. Lamb chops

d. Smoked salmon with crème fraîche

7. In Champagne bars, glasses typically hold

a. 5 ounces.

b. 3 ounces.

c. 6 ounces.

d. 4 ounces.

8. When making a toast

a. take no more than ninety seconds.

b. stand and face the audience.

c. take a sip first to calm your nerves.

d. be seated facing the toastee.

9. For the traditional toast to the bride, you'll need

a. 1 case per 100 guests.

b. 25 bottles per 100 guests.

c. 1 bottle for every 2 guests.

d. 1 bottle for every 5–7 guests.

10. The beverage most commonly overlooked when organizing big parties is

a. water.

b. beer.

c.   coffee.

d.   alcohol-free wine.

III. Check Your Success Quiz Answer Keys

Introduction to Champagne & Sparkling Wine Quiz Key

1. c

2. a

3. c

4. b

5. b

6. a

7. d

8. c

9. b

10. a

Entertaining with Champagne & Sparkling Wine Quiz Key

1. c

2. a

3. d

4. b

5. d

6. c

7. b

8. a

9. d

10. a

IV. *grape goddess Recommends*

Champagne Accessories

Wine Appreciation Guild
www.wineappreciation.com

Avant Garde Imports
www.avantgardeimports.com

Champagne Websites

Champagne Locator/Price Check
www.wine-searcher.com

Champagne Lovers Cruises
www.silversea.com

Champagne Lounges
www.bubblelounge.com

Champagne Merchant
www.dandm.com

Champagne News
www.wineloverspage.com

Champagne Sabering and the home of grape goddess!
www.planetgrape.com

V. Bibliography

Ackerman, Diane. *A Natural History of the Senses*. New York: Random House, 1990.

Brillat-Savarin, Jean Anthelme. *The Physiology of Taste, or Meditations on Transcendental Gastronomy*. Translated by M. F. K. Fisher. Washington, D.C.: Counterpoint, 1949.

Grossman, Harold. *Grossman's Guide to Wines, Beers, and Spirits*. Revised by Harriet Lembeck. Seventh revised edition. New York: Charles Scribner's Sons, 1983.

MacNeil, Karen. *The Wine Bible*. New York: Workman Publishing, 2001.

McNie, Maggie. *Champagne*. London: Faber and Faber, 1999.

Stern, Margaret. *Bagatelles from Bollinger*. New York: Margaret Stern Communications, Inc., 2003.

Sutcliffe, Serena. *Champagne: The History and Character of the World's Most Celebrated Wine*. New York: Simon and Schuster, 1988.

VI. About the Author

Meet grape goddess

Catherine Fallis is the fifth woman in the world to have earned the title of Master Sommelier. In 1997, the UK-based International Court of Master Sommeliers granted her this prestigious designation, making her one of only eleven female MSs in the world. She holds a Bachelors of Science degree from Cornell University's School of Hotel Administration.

Fallis is founder and president of planet grape, a company committed to bringing a passion for wine, food, and good living into the lives of everyday people. She is creator of the *grape goddess guides to good living*, a range of lifestyle books, seminars, and e-learning programs on wine, food, and travel, including *Wine, Champagne & Sparkling Wine, Erotic Foods,* and *Cruising.*

She is also a guest host on NBC-11 TV's *In Wine Country,* director of education for VinoVenue, and an instructor at the Culinary Institute of America, Greystone. She was introduced to wine while backpacking around Europe in her college days and honed her skills later when she returned to live in Florence and Paris. Upon her return to New York, she continued her education of wine and food in five-star houses, working with industry luminaries Alain Sailhac at Le Cirque, Leona Helmsley at the Helmsley Palace Hotel, and Kevin Zraly at Windows on the World. In 1993, she joined the harvest team with Jean-Michel Cazes and Daniel Llose at Chateaux Pichon-Baron and Lynch-Bages, in Bordeaux, France.

Since then she has designed wine programs for some of the most celebrated restaurants and resorts in the United States, including Aqua, Pebble Beach Resorts, and the Beverly Hills Hotel, and at sea for luxury liners like the *Queen Elizabeth 2* and the *Yachts of Seabourn.* She worked as wine manager for a distributor, Paradise Beverages, in Honolulu, as district manager for a supplier, Seagram Classics, covering Greater Los Angeles, and as chief retail wine buyer at Beltramo's, in Menlo Park, giving her a unique, multi-faceted perspective on the wine industry.

In addition to writing wine columns for the *San Francisco Chronicle, San Francisco Examiner, Touring and Tasting, Santé,* and numerous other publications, she is chief consulting editor for *The Encyclopedic Atlas of Wine* (Global Publishing), editor of the *Pocket Encyclopedia of Wine* (Portable Press/Advantage Publishers), has penned chapters in *The Global Encyclopedia of Wine* (Wine Appreciation Guild), *The Chalk Hill Winery Sommelier Guide to Restaurants in America* (Chalk Hill Press), *America: The Complete Story* (Global Publishing), and *Travelers' Tales.* She worked on vineyard mapping for Oz Clarke's *Wine Atlas* (Little, Brown and Company), co-edited the Beverage Testing Institute's *Guide to Buying Wine* series, and published their premiere issue of *Tastings, The Journal.*

Catherine gives frequent educational presentations to consumers and to the trade, and she volunteers her time to charitable events. She is a mentor and role model for many young men and women entering the industry, is a member of numerous wine societies, and is frequently asked to lend her palate as a wine judge. She has financially supported three foster daughters through the Childreach organization and is working towards becoming a certified foster parent. In her free time she enjoys hiking in the mountains, horseback riding, skiing, sea kayaking, and sabering champagne. A novice gardener, she is wondering how to cultivate white truffles in her backyard.

From Another Planet

For pretty much as long as I can remember, my friends and colleagues have commented that I came from another planet, so I figured I might as well call my business "planet grape" and create a cartoon character as my alter ego to boot! Who is grape goddess? She is the cartoon character I created to bring wine, food, and good living into the lives of people just like you.

grape goddess, fearless leader of planet grape

- mission statement: Bringing wine, food, and good living down to Earth

- what I do: educate Earthlings with my *grape goddess guides to good living* programs, an integral component of the *grape goddess guides to good living* media platform encompassing Internet, print, broadcast, and consumer-direct outlets

- visit planet Earth frequently, traveling on interplanetary shuttles

- able to assume human form so as not to intimidate Earthlings

- monitor Earthling activities from my Intergalactic Observation Station

- offer intergalactic customer empowerment and service from my support staff on planet Earth, the Wine Police and the Snob Squad

- *Don't make me send out the Wine Police!*

- *Don't make me send out the Snob Squad!*

grape goddess didn't fall from a shooting star:

> Wine was never a part of my life growing up on planet grape. The procreators weren't often around. Luckily, the other offspring and I had plenty of company—popular American television shows that came beaming in from the Intergalactic Observation Station—and interplanetary shuttles to planet Earth brought lots of contact with American culture. So it was that I grew up on an Earthling diet of Kool Aid, mac 'n cheese, Pringles potato chips, and Ho Hos, enjoyed with the other offspring while watching *I Love Lucy* and *Star Trek*.
>
> Growing up in some pretty rough hoods, I always thought, "There's gotta be something better than this." I started working at age twelve, and by my college days I had finally saved enough money to take an interplanetary shuttle to planet Earth, where I headed for Europe. To stretch my funds, I took overnight train rides, sleeping on the luggage racks above the seats. Bread, cheese, and, to my delight, wine, were dietary staples for even those of modest means. For the first time, I saw that wine was an integral component of the meal, rather than a cocktail, and that dining was a joyful, communal, sensually charged, and satisfying experience. From that moment, I recognized my life's calling.

Dear grape goddess

"Thank you for everything you are doing for wine. God bless you."
Robert Mondavi, Napa Valley

"You have a special gift to teach and both Vida and I learned soooooo much!!!"
Robert and Vida Clay, Charleston, South Carolina

"Catherine gave me the confidence not to feel I have to agree with all the U.S. wine magazine reviews for 'big' wines—that character, personality, and complexity count."
Skay Davidson, massage therapist, Berkeley, California

"The energy with which you devote yourself to your work is inspiring, and so is all of the creativity that comes pouring out of you. Your writing is highly descriptive and evocative."
Paul Kaihla, senior writer, *Business 2.0—Time Warner*

"Thanks to grape goddess, I am no longer intimidated by the 'wall of wines' when I go to the liquor store or confused when I am handed a wine selection menu at a restaurant!"
Erin Reynolds, 26 years old, Chicago

"Your wine pairings were the best I've had in my life!"
Robert Redford, at Aqua Restaurant, San Francisco, June 20, 2003

"Catherine, the grape goddess, encouraged me to be open and receptive to new aromas and tastes—a terrific way to learn about geography and culture."
John Nutt, Berkeley, California

"A great performance! Thank you for your expertise at Richie's 41st birthday!"
Heather Locklear, Los Angeles, California, July 11, 2001

"You are this unusual combination of quirky and refined. I loved your Champagne presentation and sabering at the Bubble Lounge!"
Marlene Anthony, Travel Specialist, San Francisco, February 18, 2004

"Wow is all I can say—such a dramatic and showy presentation! Everyone loved watching your sabering! Thank you for sharing your passion with our guests."
Stephanie Harkness, Silicon Valley Capital Club, November 1, 2003

"Your demonstration was terrific. You really know how to 'wow' the crowd."
Carissa Chappellet, Chappellet Vineyard, Napa Valley, November 7, 2003

"Catherine shows no preference for California but is familiar with wines from every continent."
***Uit* magazine, Belgium**

"Catherine is intelligent and very attractive, has a quick wit, and possesses great intrigue."
Wilfred Wong, e-Commerce Cellarmaster, Beverages and More, Concord, California

"The way you explain things makes me want to learn more."
Kathy Mintun, bartender, Aqua Restaurant

"Thank you for all your expertise and insights. You vastly improved my passion, knowledge, and professionalism."
Rodney Schick, Aqua Restaurant, San Francisco

"Catherine,
I came away from the Sommelier Summit with so many awesome experiences, but one of the ones I will carry with me the longest is listening to your words of encouragement in the back of that sweaty little plane to Paso Robles. I came home more fired up than ever to sit for my next level of tests. Thank you very much."
John Paddon, Sommelier, Commander's Palace, New Orleans

"We are so fortunate to have women like you who have forged the way into the male-dominated world of advanced wine education."
Patti Hogan, Sommelier-at-large, Seattle

"I have known Catherine for fifteen years. She was my assistant at Windows on the World. She has a great personality, has great presentation, has great ability to work with a variety of people, and does it gracefully. I have a tremendous amount of respect for her."
Kevin Zraly, president of Wine Services International, New Paltz, NY

"The power of Catherine Fallis lies in her wine tasting palate—so sharp, so precise!—and as we all know in the business, the key to a strong palate is ability to communicate. Words come as easily from Catherine Fallis as honey from the bee. There are a lot of brilliant wine professionals serving in the industry today, but few come as worldly and well spoken as Catherine. Obviously, I am one of her biggest and longtime (over ten years) fans. But as far as I know, everyone who has worked with her, or for whom she has done work, feels the same!"
Randal Caparoso, founding partner, Roy's Restaurant; winemaker; and writer

"You give people faith and courage to move forward."
Lars Ryssdal, fine wine manager, Young's Columbia Distributing, Seattle

"I get two or three calls a day about Catherine. She is just so approachable."
Michael Mina, former chef and partner, Aqua Development Corporation, San Francisco, March 20, 2002

"Your work, image, presence, and visibility have helped and inspired me so much. Thank you."
Jean Arnold-Sessions, CEO, Hanzell Vineyards, Sonoma, October 16, 2003

"You are the best."
Steven Olson, a.k.a., The Wine Geek

Catherine Fallis, MS
Planet Grape LLC
240 Lombard Street, #826
San Francisco, California, 94111
(415) 834-0784
(415) 425-5828
grapegoddess@planetgrape.com

0-595-32702-8

Printed in the United States
23571LVS00007B/286-321

9 780595 327027